A Sackful Of Plays And Poems For Christmas

A Sackful Of Plays And Poems For Christmas

By

John Coutts

Preface by General John Gowans

Robert Greene Publishing
118 Old Road East
Gravesend Kent
DA12 1PF

(Even bigger and better edition!)

1999

The songs, plays and poems in this book have been written for performance, especially in Christmas concerts and Carol Services.

'Checkpoint' has been performed on BBC Radio Kent and 'Shepherds' Encounter' adapted for RTM Radio.

Poetry by John Coutts has been performed on Scottish and BBC Television, on BBC Schools and Local Radio.

'A Lullaby' has been set to music by Adrian Lyons: 'Sing to the Lord' (Children's Voice Series, Volume 3) Salvationist Publishing and Supplies, London WC1H 9NN, 1996.

First edition 1986 - reprinted 1987, 1992
Enlarged and revised edition, 1994
Further enlarged and revised 1999

ISBN: 0 9510602 4 4

Cover design by Marion Coutts

Published by:
Robert Greene Publishing

Printed by:
ProPrint
Riverside Cottage
Great North Road
Stibbington
Peterborough PE8 6LR

THE PLAYS AND POETRY OF JOHN COUTTS

The plays and poetry of John Coutts spring, apparently painlessly, from a well-stocked mind and a well-warmed heart. There is humanity and a seeming simplicity about his verses which puts the reader dangerously at ease. I say 'dangerously' because, thus disarmed, the mind is not ready to defend itself from the sometimes piercing message or the new idea that would normally be summarily rejected. We find ourselves sharing insights and experiences with the writer and not just reading about them.

John's whimsical humour has a great deal of John Betjeman about it - and is certainly none the worse for that. His strong Christian faith cannot pass unnoticed. There is no doubt that some of his inspiration is drawn from the years spent as a Salvation Army Officer in the United Kingdom in Africa - and his more recent service in Russia and at home.

I have been a fan of John's writings for many years and always felt they deserved a wider readership. It is my hope that the publication of this '*sackful*' will provide just that.

John Gowans

CONTENTS

NOVEMBER IN ENGLAND

Lord of the drizzle, the damp and the chill;
Lord of the leaves that lie soaking and still;
Christmas comes earlier, year after year;
Santa's been sighted! Your season is here.

TV commercials proclaim the good news;
Make us an offer we dare not refuse.
Come with your credit cards: stand up and spend!
Pay when the universe comes to an end.

Lord of November, come early, come soon:
Gleam through the mist of our grey afternoon.
Short and depressing and dull is our day.
Come with the catalogues: come Lord - and stay.

SPENDING SPREE

'That was the true light, which lighteth
every man that cometh into the world.'

This Christmas business . . . really!
                    Children clutching
Expensive presents in their grubby hands;
Hot tears, smeared faces, jelly in the hair,
New playthings well and truly smashed by teatime!
Too much to eat: too many close encounters
With Santa Claus in crowded High Street stores.
Too much to drink: too loud the ringing tills
And pre-recorded bells. Can 'Silent Night' -
Relayed remorselessly from floor to floor -
Relieve your aching feet - or broken heart?
Let's close the bloated business down . . .
                    . . . and yet
A child was born alive in Bethlehem
Betrothing Then and There to Here and Now:
Outcast, a vagrant, narrowly escaping
Untimely liquidation by the state.
Such waifs are often seen on television.
We feel . . . or feel we ought to feel . . .
                              Beware!
Is that the Light that Lighteth Every Man
Shining behind the cardboard Manger Scene?
And do the children feel immortal longings
Upon them as they climb the stairs to bed?
And can we build a bright Jerusalem
Among the empty beer cans? Is it true that
God, in an act so simple and so strange,
Embarked upon a spending spree of love?

A BLESSING FOR CHRISTMAS MORNING

The slow warm wave of sleep began to move
    Silently back.
I felt the bulging bumpy sack
    Standing beside

The bed: my childish puzzled hand inspected
    Lumps, corners, shapes.
Ribbons and knotted strings and tapes -
    Odd, unexpected -

Caressed me through the swollen pillow-case.
    Suddenly, truth -
Pure - as perceived by saint or youth -
    Made my heart race.

I saw the light, as bright as noonday sun!
    He had been there!
Bringing requested gifts most rare
    To me, the one

And only Christmas child: Fumbling again,
    Still half in doubt,
My hesitating hands made out
    The clockwork train:

Key, pistons, wheels - O long-deferred desire!
    Friend, may your joy
Be, like the thanks of one small boy,
    Whole, good, entire.

CHRISTMAS 1947

(a boy's encounter with prisoners of war)

They tried to sing. It sounded more like groaning.
Each of the prisoners wore a brown or black
Battledress jacket. On the back a patch
Distinguished them from other human beings.
Two were tone-deaf. One - from the Russian front -
Wept when a toddler smiled at him . . . but why?

How could I hate - deriving biased views
Of Adolf Hitler from the Beano comic?
Mine was a lovely war. The nearest buzz-bomb
Landed in Bricket Wood a mile away . . .
It took a day of summer butterflies
To find the crater.
                When they shuffled in
I tried my first-year German out, but theirs
Differed. They stood in line: an awkward squad
In church if not in war. The preacher smiled.
They sang - or groaned - so slowly, sadly, slowly . . .
Whoever heard a noise like that before?
And then a second verse! Before the end
I recognised the tune - which was - amazing -
My far-from-favourite carol: 'Silent Night'.
When it was over, everybody clapped.
How very odd: odd as the Word Made Flesh . . .

THE OLD CARDBOARD CRIB

The cut-out shed is badly bent.
Poor tab-less Joseph totters down:
The Third Wise Man has lost his crown;
Time has been spent

And sticky tape consumed. The Lord
Wedged in his crib looks ill at ease.
A shepherd sags on well-worn knees.
Could we afford

To welcome Yule with something new?
Plastic, perhaps? That one-eared cow . . .
Can she be worth the effort now?
The time, the glue?

Beware! A long decade of dreams
Has blessed the shapes we half-condemn.
Behind our fragile Bethlehem
A candle gleams.

Therefore attend, observe, perceive.
We too are tatty, frail, absurd.
Our Christ is no mere make-believe:
This cardboard Word.

THE FACE AT THE WINDOW

Is there a single soul alive
In all this god-forsaken street?
A scratch brass band with aching feet
Will now proclaim to Cedar Drive

Glad tidings of a Saviour's birth.
One startled cat appears to care.
Suburban souls sit warm and stare
At Television News . . . of earth

Battered and bombed and hijacked till
Commercials blandly ease the pain.
'Pay us to go away again'
Thinks Second Horn - he's feeling ill . . .

But now appears a single light
High in the grim and gloomy house.
Quick as a bird, shy as a mouse
A child beholds the wondrous sight;

With small uncomprehending face
He sees the gleaming ring below.
Awaiting sound, he won't let go
That golden bear. Inspired, the bass

Booms boldly into 'First Noel'.
The drummer mutters 'Umpteenth Time!'
While Cornet mounts to heights sublime
And scales the cruel summit well.

Look up, cold-hearted, iceberg-eared!
The icon in the window frame
Should set your ashen hears aflame
As when the warning star appeared.

The child that holds the teddy bear
Calls to your mind the Son and Mother:
Look up, look down; observe each other,
In mutual wonder stand and stare.

Wise little one, the band below
Makes holy magic in the street.
The child above, dear frozen feet,
Recalls a Lord you ought to know.

RECALLED IN JOY . . .

An empty road: intimidating palm trees;
Heat and humidity: the tarmac shimmering;
Nothing on wheels in sight - my journey broken
And fifteen miles to go . . .
Exasperation soaked in perspiration . . .

But then, a still small voice, behind, below me:
'Father, sit down!' A shy and solemn child
Offers a home-made stool, unasked, unprompted,
In form and face and word entirely gentle . . .
I wield my best linguistic skills, but either
Respect for elders or my dubious accent
Puts paid to dialogue: the rest is silence.

Dear friends,

(Dear Lord and Friend - I count you in)

For some the gifts come thick and fast at Christmas:
There's gold, and frankincense, and aftershave
And myrrh, and monthly magazine subscriptions . . .
But look! I've brought a rarity to show:
One simple act of utmost innocence
Recalled in joy from thirty years ago.

AFTER CAROL SINGING

The carols were sung . . . we defrosted our fingers.
She got in my car . . . so close was that fresh
And thoughtful young face, that the memory lingers
Of intricate strife between spirit and flesh.

So I prayed, as we watched for the lights to turn yellow -
'Dear Lord - what a girl! - O if only I could . . . '
God spoke: 'She's the crown of creation, dear fellow;
But well-married men are required to be good.'

'The pop group can't come to the party on Monday.'
She said: 'And we've rushed the Nativity Play . . .
And will you help Jill with her talk for next Sunday?
She's stuck with her text and got nothing to say.

The boys will deliver the parcels - I'm certain.
We made jolly sure that they copied the list:
But you know that old woman who scowls through the curtain?
Would you mind? It's a chore. But she mustn't be missed.

Next term I must really get down to my history.
Get a bad grade in exams and you're sunk.
Some people at Christmas! To me it's a mystery!
On the end of term outing my best friend got drunk!'

Then she asked me . . . 'Just how do you focus attention
And really achieve concentration in prayer?'
Young friend, there are many distractions to mention . . .
The line of your bosom . . . the scent of your hair . . .

So the moment of truth came - in Leafywood Crescent -
After silence - long silence - young Beauty confessed
To the Ravenous Beast - O tidings unpleasant -
'It's mum . . . well . . . my mum's got a lump in her breast!'

We parted in grace, though my comfortings failed,
In her window the Christmas tree fairy stood spangled
With joy - and the Spirit cried 'Love has prevailed!'
. . . *Though the seat was still warm, and the safety belt dangled . . .*

A FEW THOUGHTS FROM JOSEPH

'Joseph went up to Judaea from the town of Nazareth in Galilee' (Luke 2:4)

At my time of life . . .
Just imagine the talk about me and my wife . . .
'So why did old Joseph get married?' they said.
'He had plenty to do in his carpenter's shed . . . '
I'd hammer a plank and keep perfectly calm
And murmur a prayer or a favourite psalm.
But some of their comments can cut like a knife
At my time of life.

At my time of life . . .
I was making a cradle with chisel and knife.
Dear Mary . . . her thoughts are as deep as a well
And cool as clear water and sweet as a bell . . .
And her soul is as quick and as bright as a bird . . .
Who can see what she sees? Who knows what she's heard?
So why should I worry if rumours are rife
At my time of life?

At my time of life . . .
Corruption is public . . . and rotten . . . and rife.
If only those Romans would get off our backs . . .
They treat us like termites and tag us for tax . . .
And what if my Mary should go into labour:
Could anyone here play the part of good neighbour?
I should have got used to confusion and strife
At my time of life.

At my time of life . . .
We'll soon be delivered from sorrow and strife:
The Good Lord has a purpose - as yet unrevealed:
I know - but my leathery lips are well sealed;
Now listen - the Kings of This World could all go -
There are secrets too sacred for Caesar to know.
I can laugh at his kettledrum, trumpet and fife
At my time of life.

At my time of life . . .
Well, we danced at our wedding - to tabor and fife.
And I've dreamt my own dream - it was ever so sweet.
I recall, I reflect, I refuse to repeat:
You ask me no questions: I tell you no lies:
But the child of my Mary could spring a surprise:
So I'm proud to be Joseph - the Man with a Wife -
At my time of life.

A WORD OF EXPLANATION FROM THE LANDLORD AT BETHLEHEM

'There was no room for them in the inn' (Luke 2:7)

The genuine case!
It's hard to be sure from the look on a face.
All kinds come and knock on the door of my inn.
We get tricksters and scroungers as crooked as sin:
But when we say 'no', we refuse with civility.
If 'yes', then we never admit liability.
Strangers from Nazareth - what could I do?
(Of course, friends, we'd never inflict them on you!)
But duty demands that we find a small space
For the genuine case.

That genuine case!
The lies they can tell are a perfect disgrace!
Dear guests, take no notice - proceed with your dinner.
My inn has a welcome for saint and for sinner.
The census! Poor Bethlehem's packed to the door'
Out there in the courtyard you can't see the floor.
He's a northerner - accent incredibly thick!
(Though that in itself doesn't prove it's a trick)
And strong arms of charity always embrace
The genuine case.

O the genuine case!
They can pocket your money and sink without trace . . .
But the woman's expecting - that's obvious enough -
And the husband's a carpenter - hands very rough.
I thought we were faced with a forcible entry.
'Not in here, lad!' says I. 'It's reserved for the gentry.'
That soon stopped him blustering - not that I blame him.
A father-to-be, first time round! Who could shame him?
'Calm down, now' - says I - 'We can always find space
For the genuine case.'

The genuine case!
I used to hunt swindlers for fun of the chase.
But now - in a crisis - we help if we're able.
I managed to find them a place in the stable:
A commonplace couple called . . . Joseph and Mary . . .
Some staff, I suspect, would be rather more wary.
But we can take care of disruptive behaviour,
It's part of my job to be godfather, saviour
Or nursemaid - forgetting religion and race -
To the genuine case.

The genuine case . . .
If he's telling the truth he's a long way from base.
I told her the baby could sleep in the manger.
. . . They're used to it, madam, there isn't much danger . . .
And all that it took was one look at his wife.
Of course, she could die on us - that's part of life.
But frankly, the house has got little to fear,
For I made our position abundantly clear:
No comeback on us - it's a gift of pure grace
To the genuine case.

A COMMENT FROM THE CAMEL-DRIVER'S MATE

'After Jesus was born in Bethlehem . . . Magi from the east came . . . to worship him.' (Matthew 2:1-2)

I'm just the camel-driver's mate
That keeps the desert fleet afloat.
It's not my fault the party's late.
(Recording angel - kindly note!)
I'm just the camel-driver's mate.

My masters made a stupid error:
They stopped in town - I thought it odd -
And asked your Herod - Lord of Terror -
To help locate the Son of God.
My masters made a stupid error.

But now - at last - they're safe inside.
Our Three Wise Men - three kings to you
Have swallowed camel-loads of pride . . .
Could such a crazy dream be true?
But now, at last, they're safe inside.

Hail to the Lord of life and light!
Our gifts have gone (it makes me wild:
I had to guard them day and night!)
To homeless Jesus - outhouse child.
Hail to the Lord of life and light!

But frankly, friends, I just don't care.
And you aren't here to kneel and pray.
You only came to stand and stare
At funny men from far away;
So frankly, friends, I just don't care.

In fact, I hope this is the place!
X marks the spot where God - or Jove -
Who spins that star in outer space -
Conceals his priceless Treasure Trove.
In fact, I hope this is the place . . .

A WORD FROM THE SCEPTICAL SHEPHERD

'When the angels had left them . . . the shepherds said . . .
'Let's go to Bethlehem and see this thing that has happened.'
(Luke 2:15)

I never went to Bethlehem.
I stayed behind to watch the sheep.
Glad tidings? - just the job for them,
But some of us were short of sleep.
I never went to Bethlehem.

The rest ran off to see the sight.
I stood alone to guard my post.
It's true - there was a kind of light
That could have been the Holy Ghost.
The rest ran off to see the sight.

They all returned, alive with joy,
Claiming an unexpected king.
A far-from-likely peasant boy . . .
I didn't have the heart to sing.
They all returned, alive with joy.

They tell me not to drift and doubt.
This poor-but-honest Prince of Peace
Has plans too big to leave me out.
Goodwill to all shall never cease.
They tell me not to drift and doubt.

Young god, so odd, here's half a prayer
From me: Let rarest grace anoint
The eyes of those who stand and stare
And always seem to miss the point.
Young god, so odd, here's half a prayer.

KING HEROD JOINS THE CAMPAIGN AGAINST LANDMINES

'When Herod realised that he had been outwitted by the Magi . . . he gave orders to kill all the boys in Bethlehem . . . who were two years old and under . . . '(Matthew 2:16)

I always acted for the best:
Succeeding to the Jewish throne
I set myself a simple test:
The People's Welfare - not my own.
I always acted for the best.

The tale you hear is largely true:
Three odd astrologers inquire
About a 'King' (I wouldn't do -
To hell with fools who play with fire!)
The tale you hear is largely true.

We planned a clean and sudden strike
To target only infant males:
Do call it murder if you like:
But what if Public Order fails?
We planned a clean and sudden strike.

When whispered rumours get to Rome
Caesar's response is rather brisk:
He burns you out of house and home,
And older girls are then at risk -
When whispered rumours get to Rome.

So let me serve as bogey still
In gospel, sermon, song and play.
Your cunning little mines can kill
More kids than Herod any day.
So let me serve as bogey still.

But spare a thought - or prayer for me:
Suppose he really was 'The One
Whom prophets said would set us free . . . '
Reflect: just what would you have done?
And spare a thought - or prayer - for me.

AT LAST! THE VIRGIN MARY AGREES TO HOLD A PRESS CONFERENCE FOR THE MODERN MEDIA

'Mary treasured up all these things and pondered them in her heart' (Luke 2:19)

Peace to you all! (How good to meet you,
Friends beyond our wildest dreaming.
What a shameful way to greet you:
Shock and screaming.)

Please forgive our lack of manners!
Talking box and shining light
Made us think of Roman banners.
Gave us a fright.

I'll gladly answer, friends - but must
I go through labour pains again?
With us such things are not discussed
In front of men.

Was it a virgin birth?
O dear!
Your shining eye and magic speakers
Dragged through time - are those the gear
Of scandal seekers?

I shared the truth with Luke, that Greek
Who wrote the gospel - also Acts.
He's a recording man - so seek
And find the facts.

I felt the angel come and go.
(Angels to us are plain as flowers)
Dear Luke wrote all you need to know
Of those strange hours.

So would you say you felt . . . impressed?
Wonder was mixed with joy and fear.
I simply said I'd do my best,
And God drew near . . .

And what did Joseph think?
To me
My man was true - he rarely spoke
But many an ox in Galilee
Wears his kind yoke.

Those kings? Fictitious?
Why go on
Yapping like dogs to kill my story?
One flower surpasses Solomon
In all his glory.

Look at the birds who never spin
Or plough or sow or reap or store:
They bless my work, and help me win
My bread - I bore

The Living Word . . .
Or so you say . . .
Suppose I *prove* the faith is true:
Will you be moved to pray - or pay?
How sad, if you

Who fly from earth to moon to earth,
Who speak across the empty skies,
Should miss the point of this good birth,
Of my sharp cries . . .

(No, no. We won't discuss the labour)
I wish you'd learn from my dear Son,
Love God, and try to like your neighbour:
For every one

Of his wise tales contains the splendid
Truth the angel shared with me:
Of man's primeval sorrow ended
A world set free.

To find the facts in Then and There
You fly to ask me When and How?
Go back and search your Everywhere -
Your here and now.

A listening box may well discover
My child in unexpected places.
So seek him out - your Lord and Lover -
In human faces.

But now - the sun begins to set.
Women have work . . . the loom . . . the well . . .
That crucifixion - no regret?
Forgive. Farewell.

THE COUNTRY-AND-WESTERN COWBOY CAROL

Caesar Augustus
The Sheriff of Rome
Drove poor Mary
Away from home.

Made sad Herod
A Big Bad Ranger.
He hired hitmen
To blow away danger.

Mr Anonymous
Ran the saloon.
Left poor Joseph
To gaze at the moon.

Caesar and Herod
And Mr Anon
Hadn't a clue
What was going on.

'Where's that Prince
Of Peace? Let's go!'
(Low-down shepherds
Were in the know.)

'Across the farmyard.
See that shed?
One small candle . . .
Mind your head . . .

Drop your weapons!
Now kneel down.
The Lord of Life
Has come to town.'

Little Lawman
Lurking here:
You shall be Lord
Of the wild frontier.

A LULLABY

(to a melody by Thomas Campion)

Jesus child, we welcome you,
Lord of life when time began.
By your birth - so strange so true -
God has given all He can.

Loving heart and voice reply
With a simple lullaby.

You have come to bring us life:
Make us happy, make us one.
Put an end to toil and strife
In a Christmas well begun.

Loving heart and voice reply
With a simple lullaby.

May my foe become my friend,
Anger sleep, resentment cease.
By your crib let troubles end:
You have come to bring us peace.

Loving heart and voice reply
With a simple lullaby.

A CAROL

Dear Lord of the manger, young Christ of the cold,
We bring neither silver, nor myrrh, nor fine gold:
We come not as Wise Men who bow to a king:
Across the long centuries - what can we bring?

King Herod the Cruel - some call him the Great -
Had plans to destroy you and safeguard the state.
We know the resentments that drove him to slay:
Grant healing, and show us just how we should pray.

For Caesar Augustus, the maker of kings,
Poor people were useful expendable things.
And so your dear mother was barred from the inn.
We want to learn loving: Lord help us begin.

For childhood's new dream brightest colours we use.
Our clumsy attempts we are glad you can use.
Yours too the brave hopes and strong passions of youth.
Fulfil them in wisdom: perfect them in truth.

The shabbiest presents we know you will prize.
Forgive us old folly, and do not despise
Our drab disappointments, our well-worn despair:
Renew our tired sympathy: strengthen our prayer.

And now, as the shepherds come in from the night,
We enter the stable: how dim is the light
That shows you in slumber: accept us each one.
Young Lord of all ages, our joy has begun.

THE CHILD IN NEED

(A prayer - and a response)

God of unimagined space
Far beyond our deepest dreaming:
Now we see Your glory gleaming
In a homeless baby's face:
Can so strange a plan succeed?
- *Welcome, Jesus, child in need.*

Word eternal, known at last:
Answer plainly when we doubt you;
Should we try to live without you -
Stay beside us: heal our past . . .
'Lord, we love . . . ' is all our creed.
- *Welcome, Jesus, child in need!*

Holy Spirit, see us here
(Thoughts adrift, and motives mixed)
Let our frail desires be fixed
On the love that conquers fear:
Set us free from guilt and greed.
- *Welcome, Jesus, child in need.*

God the Father, Spirit, Son;
May your broken world be mended,
Pain relieved, and foes befriended
By a Christmas well begun.
Make us glad in word and deed.
- *Welcome, Jesus, child in need.*

A PRAYER

before the icon of the Virgin and Child
'Showing the way'

'Show us the way,
Young Lord, we pray.'
'Freely you get, so freely give!'
My words direct you: read, obey . . . and live.'

'How can we know
Which way to go
When hope grows cold and fears lie deep?'
'I am the shepherd boy who loves the sheep.'

'How will it end?
And where?' *'Look, friend . . .*
The lilies neither toil nor spin.
I am the Way. You see? Shall we begin?'

A PRAYER FOR CHRISTMAS EVE . . .

Lord, you were with us here
Throughout the anxious year
Not far away -
Though fractious fear and doubt
Conspired to turn you out:
Through every hasty, hurrying day
You stood your ground - unseen, yet always near.

Soon we shall say
Unlikely King, come in!
On Christmas Eve we wait
To celebrate
The Word made new-born flesh . . . and bone and skin.
Young Prince of Peace, you have a world to win.

Mysterious God, you live
Beyond our dearest dreams - our deepest thought;
And yet we glimpse you in a human face.
Come, Lord, to grace
Our humdrum here and now, and give
Wisdom to work and wonder as we ought . . .
. . . Welcome to this holy, happy place.

A CHRISTMAS EVE CONFESSION

at the Church of John the Warrior, in Moscow on January 6th, 1991 - when Christmas was celebrated in public for the first time since the Russian Revolution.

What are you telling him, solemn and slender,
Scarved in sincerity, shielding your face?
Happy the priest whose attentions are tender . . .
Is it perplexity, doubt, or disgrace?

Did you let grumbles get out of proportion?
Quarrels in quarters collective run wild?
Climb on the sorry-go-round of abortion?
Shove a poor babushka, shout at a child?

What are you whispering, Father-on-duty,
Earnest and urgent, adorning the Word?
Candles and choristers, cunning in beauty,
Hallow your counselling, seen but unheard,

What am I thinking, as worshippers jostle?
Those who see God must be flawless in heart!
Grant me, young woman, unwitting apostle,
Crumbs of contrition before I depart.

Lord of nativity, Light Unexpected,
Down the grey streets muffled Muscovites go.
Hear a poor prayer for that idol neglected:
Lenin impenitent, powdered in snow.

PROJECTS OFFICE

(Funds to assist to provide Christmas cheer for
the elderly have been sent to a West African city.
Now a report must be recorded and sent to the
donors . . .)

To Projects Office, PO Box, etcetera.

'Dear Sir,
The grant you gave was used as follows:
We purchased thirty plastic bags. In each
We placed a pound of rice, some tea, dried beans,
St Matthew's gospel in the local language,
Sugar and salt, a box of matches, tinned
Tomato puree, local leaves resembling
Spinach, bananas, oranges, some palm
Oil, and a greeting card.'

New paragraph.

'The funds, we trust, were wisely spent: the list
Of aged people checked and double-checked
For fear of fraud. The bags were packed on Christmas
Eve, and taken round by volunteers
On Christmas Day. Each team included one
Person who spoke the local language. I
Myself took part . . . '

The speaker stops dictating.

Old woman, please forgive!
We came to help. I never knew your home
Was bare, so very bare; the walls unpainted
Concrete: never thought we'd scare you stiff,
We strangers bearing gifts. You saw and dreaded
My whitish face and khaki shorts, my thin
Thin lips and pointed nose. Was it Police?
Or Taxmen? Trouble - yes, official trouble!
We gave you such a fright on Christmas morning
Attempting to deliver one of thirty
Plastic bags containing . . . never mind . . .

For once you understood, you gave us thanks
In long melodious words and solemn gestures
Centuries old. You greeted Khaki Shorts
(Who hardly knows the local language) kindly,
Maternally, a queen beside your charcoal
Fire: then you smiled and made your farewell curtsey
Slowly and gently, being old, but smoothly,
As though the years had spared your maidenhood
You blessed me then. We went our way unsnubbed
And you unpatronised.
Let's try again.

And so back to the dictation . . .

To Projects Office, PO Box, etcetera:

'Dear Sir,
The grant you gave was used as follows . . . '

STANDARD REPORT ON ANY DISASTER

We've got the death rate down to ten percent.
This, you may feel, is ten percent too many.
But thank you, friends, for every pound and penny..
Be sure your gifts are well and wisely spent.

Perhaps you wonder where the money went?
We try to reach the place of greatest need
With grain and powdered milk. So kind *read*
The interim report I now present.

Those media comments we may well resent.
'Poor paperwork and misdirected pity'
Appears a sad reward for your committee,
Which welcomes queries if sincerely meant.

It's Christmas, friends . . . a long way off from Lent.
But why not spare a prayer, or stop and think,
Forego a little food, a drop of drink,
And make today a truly great event?

I call you all to holy discontent.
Let's get the death rate down from ten . . . to five . . . ?
May sleepy children rest in peace, alive,
And mother's lullaby replace lament.

BUSINESS AS USUAL

(a true story from Lagos, Nigeria)

Twisted, distorted beggar man!
He crawls with clogs on hands and knees.
Observe his features if you can.
Improve his prospects as you please.
Here is a thing a saint would hiss . . .
Young Son of God, you came for this.

The office workers hurried out;
The office workers hurried in.
Could they avoid that crouching tout?
Their pennies hit - or missed - his tin.
Young Jesus, blessed by Mary's kiss -
Could you be born for such as this?

Believers planned a Christmas feast,
And did the true disciple's duty,
Calling the lone, the lame, the least
To come and share donated booty.
A fleeting taste of endless bliss . . .
Who dares, dear Lord, to sneer at this?

The crooked beggar answered 'No!
Today of days I make the most.'
- He smiled a gentle smile - 'And so
I simply daren't desert my post.
The trade is far too good to miss,'
Lord, did you die to deal with this?

THE SOUND OF MUSIC

Remember 'The Sound of Music'?
That film with 'do-re-mi'?
Vivacious Julie Andrews
Delightful to hear and see?

Von Trapps - that Holy Family -
Were driven to run away
Or sing for Adolf Hitler,
And sell their souls for pay.

Remember the scene that caught them
Cold in the headlights glare?
Gestapo agents shouting
'Freeze! Just hold it here!'

They froze indeed - and mighty dread
Did seize their troubled mind.
Bad tidings of great hate were brought
To them and all mankind.

So was it like that by Bethlehem?
'Hold it, shepherds, freeze!'
Someone or something luminous
Leaving them weak at the knees?

Drilled by a laser beam of light?
Caught on the cruel hop?
Itching, twitching, squinting,
Wanting the joke to stop?

Blinking in bewilderment,
Wondering 'What the hell?'
'Don't panic, lads!' - that Something said.
'Glad tidings I do tell.

It isn't 'beggar your neighbour',
Or 'Glory to be Greed!
It's 'Unto-us-a-child-is-born' -
Now there's the news you need.

It's not 'Hurrah for Herod!'
Or 'Romans rule, OK!'
It's just a vagabond infant,
Economically wrapped in hay.

A social call in Bethlehem
Should deal with any doubt;
Go, shepherds, go - with attitude -
And quickly check it out!'

Cue in the Sound of Music.
Cross fade the Heavenly Chorus!
Fast forward through the centuries . . .
Beware what lies before us.

Beware of Ethnic Cleansing,
With droves of refugees:
Beware of Global Warming
- You either fry or freeze.

Beware of Nuclear Fallout;
In case it lands on you . . .
Father, forgive our follies:
We know not what we do.

Rewind the tape to Bethlehem:
Where else can sinners go?
Freeze-frame the Christ in close-up:
Be still, dear friends and know . . .

The light is warm and gentle.
Remove your shades - if any -
This child is like no other.
This child is one of many.

The only radiation here
Is God's intensive grace:
It pierces mind and marrow
Through time and thought and space.

So fade the angry hubbub
Of hateful hell - and cue
The sound of silent music.
I hear it, friends . . . can you?

GROWING

Jesus said: 'Consider the lilies of the field . . . ' (Matthew 6:28)

First a seedling
Falls asleep.
Then a root
Burrows deep.
Now a shoot
Greeny-white
Curls and twirls
Towards the light.

Tendrils creep
Down below;
Stem and branches
Breathe and grow.
Leaves alive
Sway and thrive:
Water, air
And earth prepare . . .

Now the flower
Pale and blue
Enjoys her hour:
And so can you . . .

BILLY'S BRIGHT IDEA

O brave Christmas morning!
O sight for young eyes!
Young Billy the Boy
Had a splendid surprise.

A sock full of treats!
A sack full of toys,
A day full of treats,
A parcel of joys!

Time passed, as it must . . .
Yet Bill was at ease;
For school was far distant
So do as you please . . .

Dear sweet television!
Could life be made better?
Then mother said, 'How
About writing a letter

To kind Uncles George
And Alan, and Aunt
Rebecca, to thank them . . . ?'
He rudely said 'Shan't!

The worst thing at Christmas
It spoils the whole season -
Is letters of thanks!
Is there any good reason

Why Bill should sit down
And say he's So Grateful
To Aunt after Aunt?
There's already a plateful

Of programmes to watch
And games to be played.
Uncle George and the others
Must wait - I'm afraid . . .'

But then Billy thought
Of something far better . . .
'Could I send my kind friends
A circular letter?

As soon as we've printed
A few year's supply
We can quickly *cross out*
that which does not apply.

'Dear Sir (Or 'Dear Madam')
I really must thank
You for thoughtfully sending
A beautiful' *(Blank*

Space to be filled)
In addition I got
From Uncle/Aunt/Cousin
A . . . *dot . . . dot . . . dot . . . dot . . .*

For my birthday I'd like . . .
(Leave several lines here)
And I hope you enjoy
A happy new year . . .

This page has run out,
So I really must end,
Your affectionate nephew,
(Child, cousin, chum, friend)'

What a wonderful scheme!
The best thing to come
From young Master Bill,
But a misguided mum

Rejected it roughly,
And made him sit down
With pen and with paper,
With moan, groan and frown,

And write without stopping
Epistles - one dozen -
To all those dear aunts,
And to each jolly cousin.

In vain he opposed
Such a cruel decision!
In vain he demanded
To watch television . . .

'Jackanory . . . ', 'Blue Peter . . . '
Those programmes went by -
'I had wanted to see' -
He complained with a sigh -

'Captain Pugwash - of course:
Then come back again
After eating my tea,
To that film with John Wayne . . .

But just for these letters
The Universe stops,
And I shan't get a look in
At 'Top of the Pops'.'

Then he threw down his ball-point.
'It's finished at last.
The letters are written,
The nightmare is past.

My hands are all inky:
My brain is half dead.'
'Get washed, then' - said mother -
'And straight into bed.'

BEAUTY AND THE SANTA

Albert Y Grumble's
Job was a bore.
He played Santa Claus
In a huge crowded store.

His beard was too tickly,
His robe was too hot.
And most of the children
Disliked what they got.

His grotto and reindeer
Were meant to look funny,
But mums would complain
About value for money,

And the children declared
(If compelled to give thanks)
'The Santa was better
At Boojum and Banks.'

Then the manager said
(In a manager's voice)
'We can't have a glum
Father Christmas! Rejoice,

Friend Albert! This firm
Won't employ the unwilling!
Our girls at the counter -
Whose feet may be killing

Them - constantly smile
At grumpy and snooty
Customers. Santa,
Get back to your duty!'

Greasy sausage for lunch!
Our Bert felt still sicklier,
His robe even hotter,
His beard even ticklier.

He had to face up
To those Dear Girls and Boys
While canned 'Silent Night'
Made continuous noise . . .

So he shook up his sack
And wished he were dead,
But failed to observe
A small Someone who said

'You poor Father Christmas!
I know you're not real.
Your beard is on crooked.
How hot you must feel!

Give me any old present,
And I'll give you this!'
To our Albert's surprise
He got a quick kiss,

All tingly and sweet
In spite of the beard:
Then that fairy - or angel -
At once disappeared.

'Please make me a good
Father Christmas again!'
Said Bert - as he prayed
For Goodwill Towards Men,

Not even excluding
The Manager, who
Gets cross before Christmas
With so much to do -

But never gets kissed -
Not once in a while -
By the girls with sore feet
Who ceaselessly smile.

CHECKPOINT

An interlude for Christmas

Characters Soldier A
Soldier B
Joseph
Mary

The play takes place at a checkpoint on the road to Bethlehem. It can be simply staged at a carol service or other Christmas event.

Two soldiers come in and erect a barrier. They stamp and rub their hands to keep warm.

Soldier A Cold enough for you?

Soldier B Cold enough for most people. I hate this job.
Not what soldiering's all about.

Soldier A You make a bit on the side don't you!
Guarding the road in the Emperor's name.
Collecting tolls at a penny a traveller.

Soldier B They need our protection, don't they? It's
funny how grateful they are.

Soldier A Here's a couple coming now. What do you
make of them? That woman's worn out. The
man's got to carry her.

Soldier B Wife and child: that's what he's carrying.

Soldier A You won't get much out of *this* pair.

Soldier B Just a bit of fun. Leave them to me.

Joseph and Mary come forward. They stop at the barrier. At last Joseph plucks up courage to speak.

Joseph May we pass through - if you don't mind?

Soldier B State your name, occupation, place of origin and proposed destination.

Joseph Joseph of Nazareth. Carpenter by trade. Travelling to Bethlehem. With my wife Mary.

Soldier B Produce your certificate of registration.

Joseph We don't have one yet. That's why we're on our way to Bethlehem. To register for the census.

Soldier B In view of the state of emergency civilian personnel are not allowed to pass any military checkpoint except upon production of a valid certificate of registration.

Joseph But unless I pass the checkpoint I can't get one.

Soldier A Register at home, Mr Carpenter. Register at home. Save us all time and trouble.

Joseph But I'm not allowed to register at home. I have to go back to my place of birth. I was born in Bethlehem. But I live in Nazareth. Up north. In Galilee. I'm really doing my best to comply with all the official regulations.

Soldier A Did you say *Galilee*, Mr Carpenter? Galilee is a hotbed of terrorism. We've served in Galilee - we know. We're on the look-out for Judas *the Galilean* and his gang.

Joseph Do I look like a terrorist?

Soldier A Cheeky, aren't we?

There is a pause.

Joseph I can't pass the checkpoint unless I produce a certificate of registration, and I can't get a certificate of registration unless I pass the checkpoint.

Soldier B That's your problem.

Joseph It's absurd!

Soldier B Life . . . is absurd.

Joseph But . . . my wife . . .

Soldier A Ah yes . . . your wife . . . come forward, woman . . .

Joseph Leave her alone. You can see her condition.

Soldier B We certainly can. And it could be a terrorist trick . . .

Joseph In the name of common humanity . . .

Soldier A There *is* no common humanity.

Joseph and the soldiers stand motionless. Mary speaks to the audience.

Mary Those men are right. It could be just a trick.
I might have come to lure them to their deaths.
Worse deeds have been and are and will be done
By women - even by expectant mothers.
You know it well enough - so look at me,
Dear far-off friends who hear my story year
By year - who mix me up with Father Christmas,
Rank me with robins, garland me with holly,
Assume I always have a helpful donkey . . .
The men who block my way are common men;
Not brutes, not beasts, not cruel for their kind.
They do not build the barriers in the mind.

The soldiers speak again . . .

Soldier A What do you reckon?

Soldier B If she dies on us, we could be in big trouble.

Soldier A Natives run screaming to the governor. Brutal treatment of pregnant woman. The high-ups won't want to know.

Soldier B But in view of the state of emergency civilian personnel are not allowed . . .

Soldier A They won't be picked up. Bethlehem's crowded. May as well let 'em through . . .

Soldier B Right. Just watch this. *(To Joseph)* Come forward, my good man. Now, what do you say about the terrorists who lurk in your native land of Galilee?

Joseph I don't say anything about them, sir.

Soldier B Well, you *should* say something about them. You should condemn them as 'enemies of the Roman Empire and the human race.'

Joseph Of course, sir. I'm loyal to Caesar, sir. 'Enemies of the Roman Empire and the human race.'

Soldier B And if you mention the name of Caesar you should of course refer to him as 'Mighty Caesar'.

Joseph Of course, sir. How silly of me. 'Mighty Caesar.'

Soldier B Louder!

Joseph 'Mighty Caesar!'

Soldier B One more try!

Joseph *(Shrieking)* 'Mighty Caesar!'

Soldier B At great personal inconvenience and purely out of sympathy with your wife we will now allow you to pass through the barrier.

Soldier A Register at Bethlehem without delay.

Joseph Of course, sir . . . Perhaps I'll be able to show you the certificate on the return journey . . .

Soldier A Are you very mad or very cheeky?

Joseph I beg your pardon?

Soldier A With or without your certificate of registration we don't want to see you again.

Soldier B Just give a donation to the soldiers' welfare fund.

He rattles a tin.

Joseph Of course. Thank you very much indeed.

He puts money into the tin.

Most kind of you. Thank you very much.

Mary and Joseph pass the barrier.

Soldier B May the gods go with you, madam. If it's a boy, don't train him to come and back and kill us, will you?

The soldiers turn their backs.

Mary They let us pass. We go our way in peace -
Or semi-peace. You know the rest already.
The inn is full of course. My time will come
In some decrepit shed or shack or shanty.
Yet many births are far more crude and bitter
Than this of mine. The weight is O-so-heavy

Now. The Lord of Glory slows me down; the love
That moves the unimagined stars lies hidden
Here in my womb. He gives me cramp. Amen.
So be it. Happy birth is always blessing.
This birth is blessing far beyond all hope.
The men who man the checkpoint cannot guess it.
They let me pass in fear and self-concern;
Perhaps a little pity. Just a little.
Their grace will do. Their grace will have to do.
Dear friends, we go to Bethlehem for you.

She and Joseph go on.

SING A SONG OF CHRISTMAS

by John Coutts

'In every youthful face I see
The Christ child smiling down on me'

(Catherine Baird - 'Reflections')

The Cast: Roving Reporter
Three Angels
Three Shepherds
Three Wise Men
Everychild
Joseph and Mary

(This interlude uses the tune of the nursery rhyme 'Sing a Song of Sixpence'. It links the traditional elements of a Nativity Play - angels, shepherds and kings - with the needs of children in today's world.)

A very large parcel is discovered on stage. Roving Reporter enters, with a microphone

Reporter Hullo there, listeners! This is your favourite radio personality - the one and only Roving Reporter. I'm here to investigate a sensation in *Anytown* . . . A large unidentified object has been discovered on stage at . . . in . . . yes . . . here it is . . . Listeners, have no fear! Your Roving Reporter is here . . . The unidentified object looks like a large Christmas parcel . . . Shall I open it?

The Audience Yes . . . Go ahead . . .

Reporter Listen . . . I hear music . . .

The tune 'Sing a Song of Sixpence' is heard.

This could be risky but I can't help it . . . it's that magic music . . . Irresistible. I'll just have to open the parcel . . .

He opens the parcel. As the music plays the angels come out of the parcel . . . the choir . . . or a solo voice . . . then sings:

Sing a song of Christmas; did you ever see
A parcel full of angels - sent to you and me:
When the parcel's opened, every angel sings:
Isn't that a funny way to praise the King of Kings?

Reporter — Well, how about that . . . ? Amazing. My first big break . . . an interview with an angel . . . Now, your highness (If that's how you speak to an angel) Do you have a message for our listeners? We have certified listening figures of umpteen million . . .

Angel 1 — *Do not be afraid. I bring you good news of great joy that will be for all the people.*

Angel 2 — *Today in the town of David a saviour has been born to you. He is Christ the Lord.*

Angel 3 — *This will be a sign to you. You will find a baby wrapped in clothes and lying in a manger . . .*

The Angels sing:

Glory in the highest: yes it's really true
God has got some happiness - wrapped up for you . . .
Joy be with you, people - peace shall never end.
Come along to Bethlehem - let Jesus be your friend:

Reporter — I'm racking my brains, listeners, but I seem to think I've heard this story before years ago, when I used to go to Sunday

School. In fact the whole thing rather reminds me of those pretty pictures you sometimes get on Christmas cards. I wonder if there are any more extra-terrestrials in that box?

The Angels sing, perhaps with choir and audience:

Is the parcel empty? Let's look inside
Shepherds don't be shy - there's no need to hide.
'Glory in the highest' - wasn't that the song?
You were first to hear the news so kindly come along . . .

And now the Shepherds emerge from the parcel

Reporter — A group of shepherds . . . well, that's certainly traditional. Would you like to make a comment, sir?

Shepherd 1 — *Suddenly a great company of the heavenly host appeared, praising God and saying:*

Shepherd 2 — *'Glory to God in the highest, and on earth peace, goodwill towards men . . . '*

Shepherd 3 — *Let's go to Bethlehem and see this thing that has happened which the Lord told us about . . .*

Reporter — Thank you very much . . . have a good trip.

The Shepherds sing:

Glory in the highest - peace on earth below:
That's the happy news that we want you all to know.
Peace be with you people - love shall never end:
Here's the King of Everywhere who wants to be your friend.

Reporter — Well, that seems to be it. It seems that we have here a repeat of the traditional Christmas story which many of you will know from school days . . . Now I think I can guess what comes next . . . Could it be those *three*

Audience . . . *Wise Men . . . !*

Reporter It is . . . !

The theme tune plays. As the Three Kings come out of the parcel. Then the Angels, Shepherds, and everybody else sing together:

Sing a song of Christmas: I wonder where they are?
Kings from somewhere faraway who saw a special star.
Gold and myrrh and frankincense - we do not need to bring:
Just a loving heart will do to set before the king.

Reporter And now, Mr Wise, would you care to comment?

First Wise Man *Where is the one who has been born king of the Jews?*

Second Wise Man *We saw his star in the east . . .*

Third Wise Man *. . . and we've come to worship him . . .*

Reporter I can give you an answer right now . . . Your king is born 'in Bethlehem in Judaea', that's it . . . Am I right?

Audience Yes!

The Shepherds, Angels and Wise Men sing:

Angels, kings and shepherds - you can see us here:
Keep us on your Christmas cards - post us every year:
Don't forget the trimmings - don't avoid the fun:
Now the parcel's empty so . . . God bless us everyone:

Reporter Well, there you have it, folks . . . I reckon the parcel's empty now . . . No bomb scare . . . no aliens from outer space . . .

no big sensation . . . just a few children
giving us the dear old Nativity Play . . .
And I guess that's all . . .

But now Everychild comes out of the parcel

Everychild O not, it's not!

Reporter Excuse me, who are you?

Everychild They call me *Everychild.*

Reporter But who on earth is *Everychild?*

Everychild *Don't you know me: Everychild?*
Good or greedy, tame or wild?

I'm the boy from long ago,
Hunting deer with spear and bow.

I'm the girl from far away:
Be a sport - come out to play!

I'm behind your garden wall:
Could you let me have my ball?

I am the wise and winning one:
Fab at games and full of fun.

I went missing, were you there?
I was Taken Into Care.

I am brown or white or black:
I lie ill on mother's back,

Far too weak for treats or tricks . . .
I have legs like brittle sticks:

Sometimes I'm a perfect pest.
On the whole, I do my best.

Did you see me on TV?
Will you take me on your knee?

I'm the reason Jesus came.
Don't you dare forget my name . . .

Good or greedy, tame or wild,
Any child is Everychild.

Reporter — But Everychild, you aren't mentioned in the Bible, are you? How on earth did you get into the show?

Everychild — Of course Everychild is in the Bible. I'm mentioned over and over again . . . It says 'See that you do not look down on one of these little ones . . . whoever welcomes one of these little ones in my name welcomes me'.

(Matthew 18:21; Mark 9:37)

Everychild sings:

Sing a song of Christmas - Everychild is here . . .
Charity shall bless you - and wipe away your fear:
Smile if you should see me: don't forget my name.
All for love of Everychild is just why Jesus came.

Reporter — (Baffled) Yes . . . well . . . thank you very much . . . Your very own Roving Reporter has solved the mystery . . . and now . . . well . . . back to the studio . . .

Everychild — Haven't you forgotten someone else . . . The star of the show? The Lord of Glory?

Mary and Joseph enter, bearing the child Jesus, the rest of the actors kneel . . . At last, rather reluctantly, Roving Reporter kneels too.

And then everyone sings:

Sing a song of Christmas - everybody sing . . .
Bring your best intentions to set before the King.
Faith and hope shall lead you - guide you on your way
Now the Lord of love and life has really come to stay.

A prayer or carol may follow.

SHEPHERDS' ENCOUNTER

An interlude for Christmas

Characters	Jacob Daniel Benjamin (Shepherds) Miriam (A Mad Woman)

On the road to the stable at Bethlehem: Jacob and Daniel enter in high excitement. They do not see Mad Miriam.

Jacob — Benjamin's not here. Better not wait.

Daniel — Give him a moment. Try a tune on your pipe. That'll fetch him.

Jacob — I'm going to give my pipe to the new king, Daniel. Play it first, though *(He tries a few notes)* How about that?

Daniel — Not quite as good as the heavenly choir.

Jacob — Out there in the fields, when the light began to shine. I couldn't believe it. And the voice! 'Glory to God . . . and peace on earth . . . ' Was it all a dream? Did it happen?

Daniel — A dream come true, if you ask me.

Jacob — So what's your gift to the king then, Daniel? Let's have a look?

Daniel — It's a silver shekel of Judas the Maccabee. Dates back to the days when we had our freedom. It's been in our family for generations.

Jacob — This new king they told us about - the one that's born in Bethlehem. Maybe he'll do better than Judas the Maccabee. Wipe out all the Romans.

Daniel That's enough of that, Jacob. Dangerous talk. Here's our Benjamin now.

Benjamin runs in.

Benjamin Here I am. Sorry to keep you. I had to get it. Ran all the way home for it.

Jacob Get what?

Benjamin This quilt. A patchwork quilt. My present for the king. Grandmother made it . . . Come on, then, let's got going . . . Hey, who's this?

Daniel Dear oh dear. Mad Miriam. The beggar woman. What's she doing here?

Benjamin Poor soul.

Jacob They say she used to be really good looking. Never got married though. Some fellow wanted her. But she didn't want him. So he went and bought love powder from an Assyrian doctor. Put it in her porridge. Too strong. Burnt her brains out. So he never got what he wanted and she's been like that ever since. Hardly ever speaks.

Benjamin Daniel, is that true?

Daniel Who knows? Could be the Romans. When they cleaned up Judaea ten years ago. *They* didn't use love powder, that's for certain. Come on, lads, never mind Mad Miriam. Whoever hurt her it wasn't us. Remember what the angel said:

'To you in David's town this day
Is born of David's line
A Saviour, who is Christ the Lord,'

Benjamin 'And this shall be the sign:
The heavenly babe you there shall find
To human view displayed . . . '

Miriam 'All meanly wrapped in swaddling bands,
And in a manger laid.'

Benjamin *(Amazed)* She can speak! How did she know that? Who told her?

Jacob They're like that. Mad people. They *know* things. Like the prophets in the Bible. Some of them were half mad.

Daniel Maybe she was out in the fields, like us. Anything could happen on a night like this. Come on, lads, on we go to Bethlehem.

Daniel and Jacob go out.

Benjamin How did you know? How on earth did you know what the angel said to us? I'm not angry. I won't hurt you.

She makes signs, asking for food.

Something to eat? Is that it? All right. Here's a piece of bread. Tomorrow's breakfast. That's what it is. Eat it . . . Go on . . .

She eats the bread.

. . . a night to dream of. A sky full of light. Angels . . . you can't describe it . . . Warm and wonderful . . . feels colder now . . . Go on. Have another piece.

She eats more bread.

Love powder? Was that it? Did someone give you too much love powder - and hurt you? In your head, like?

No reply.

Maybe that was just Jacob talking. He *would* think of love powder. More likely the Romans. You know . . . the Romans . . . soldiers . . . like this!

He uses his crook like a soldier's pike, pointing it at her

(Shouting) Halt! Who goes there?

But Miriam is terrified. She shrieks and staggers back with outstretched arms.

Look, I'm terribly sorry. I didn't mean to scare you. Honestly. It's not a pike. Just a harmless little shepherd's crook. I'm a fool. That's what I am . . . Look, have some dates. Sweet dates. The rest of my breakfast. Please . . .

She shakes her head - arms still outstretched.

Crucified, was it? Romans crucified somebody. You saw them do it. Someone you loved? I'm sorry. Ever so sorry. Go on. You have the dates. Eat them all up.

She takes the dates and starts to eat.

You're shivering. I gave you a shock. Oh dear. I feel cold too now. It was so warm out there in the fields when the great light shone. What's this you're after?

She tugs at his patchwork quilt.

My quilt. Sorry. You can't have that. It's a present. For someone special. For the new king. I can't let you have it. My granny made it.

But she goes on tugging.

I know you're cold, Miriam. And I'm sorry I frightened you. But this quilt . . . it's special . . . Oh well, I suppose I've got to make it up to you somehow . . . God forgive me for scaring you. And God forgive me for . . . giving you this . . . there you are . . . It's really warm.

He wraps the quilt round her. She speaks at last.

Miriam	My curses on King Cruelty.
His eyes are dull and dead.
His guards are armed with anger;
He rules the land of dread.

Benjamin	What's that? I don't understand.

Miriam	Love to the Lord of Nowhere
Whom nothing can destroy.
He and his friends from Everywhere
Shall share the land of joy.

Benjamin	What on earth is she talking about?

Miriam	My blessing on the shepherd
Who keeps me from the cold.
May heart's desire come home to him
Before his dreams grow old.

Jacob returns.

Jacob	Come along, Benjamin. It's marvellous. A kind of cave. A man and his wife and a baby. It's . . . nothing . . . and it's . . . everything. I gave him my pipe. Daniel's given him the silver shekel of Judas the Maccabee. It's a sign. A sure sign that we'll win our freedom.

Benjamin	She said something. I don't know what she said but she said something.
Jacob	Who did?
Benjamin	Mad Miriam.
Jacob	Why on earth is she wearing your blanket?
Benjamin	I just gave it her. And my breakfast. She needs it, doesn't she?
Jacob	Man, you're a fool. You've gone and given your granny's quilt to mad Miriam. You've got nothing left for the Messiah.
Benjamin	I know why she's mad. It wasn't your love powder. The Romans hurt her.
Jacob	The Prince of Peace is born at last. We're invited and you miss out . . .
Benjamin	I can still go if I like . . .
Jacob	Not if you've got nothing to give.
Miriam	I wish for newest children Who face the faceless years, No hatred in their laughter; No terror in their tears. I pray for all good people With nothing left to give. O go and give your nothing, And learn to love and live.

Benjamin — I told you she was talking. God does speak through crazy people. But I can't understand her . . .

Jacob — All I got hold of was 'Go!' She *did* say go. Come on, Benjamin. I'll take you to the stable. You've got nothing to give so you'll just have to smile . . .

He takes Benjamin out: But Benjamin still looks back.

Miriam — For once the King of Everywhere
Has bound the Lord of Dread,
Your nothing shall be everything;
Your stone shall turn to bread.

HELPFUL SUGGESTIONS!

I need breakfast - I need bed -
I need a kiss for a bump on my head -

I need Krinkly Krunkly chips -
I need a space ship for afternoon trips -

I need the latest top cassettes -
I need dad - to mind my pets -

I need a pencil - I need mum -
I need the answer to a horrible sum -

I need a jumbo ice-cream cone -
I need a private bully-free zone -

I need a dream that's gotta come true -
I need the Universe - I need *You!*